Twenty
EXPLORERS

Andrew Langley

Illustrated by Edward Mortelmans

Twenty Names

Editor: Rosemary Ashley

First published in 1988 by
Wayland (Publishers Limited)
61 Western Road, Hove
East Sussex BN3 1JD, England

British Library Cataloguing in Publication Data
Langley, Andrew
   Twenty names in exploration.
   1. Exploration, to 1985 – Biographies –
   For children
   I. Title   II. Mortelmans, Edward, *1915–*
   910'.92'2

   ISBN 1–85210

Phototypeset by Kalligraphics Ltd, Redhill, Surrey
Printed in Italy by G. Canale C.S.p.A., Turin

Contents

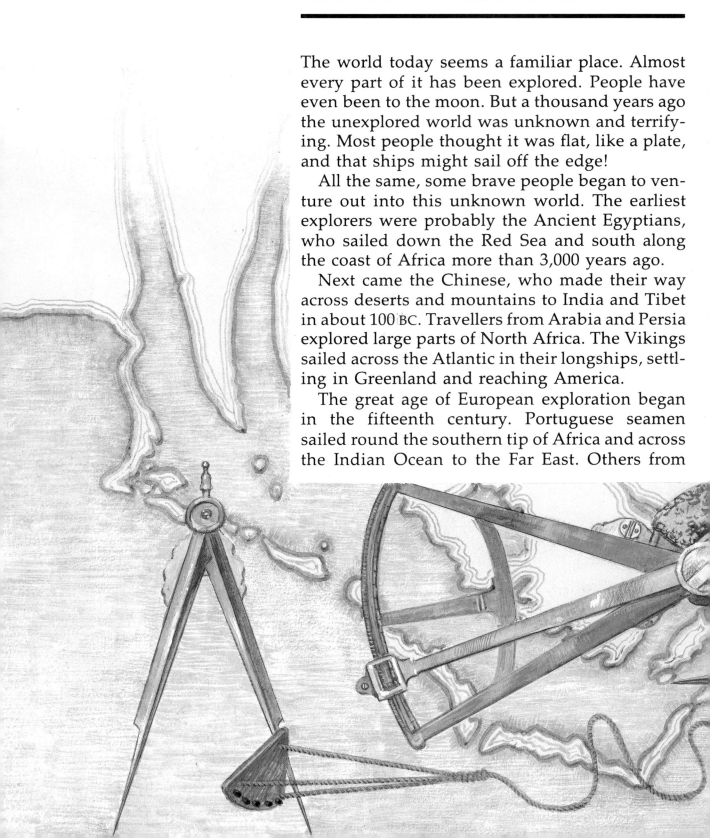

Quest for the unknown

The world today seems a familiar place. Almost every part of it has been explored. People have even been to the moon. But a thousand years ago the unexplored world was unknown and terrifying. Most people thought it was flat, like a plate, and that ships might sail off the edge!

All the same, some brave people began to venture out into this unknown world. The earliest explorers were probably the Ancient Egyptians, who sailed down the Red Sea and south along the coast of Africa more than 3,000 years ago.

Next came the Chinese, who made their way across deserts and mountains to India and Tibet in about 100 BC. Travellers from Arabia and Persia explored large parts of North Africa. The Vikings sailed across the Atlantic in their longships, settling in Greenland and reaching America.

The great age of European exploration began in the fifteenth century. Portuguese seamen sailed round the southern tip of Africa and across the Indian Ocean to the Far East. Others from

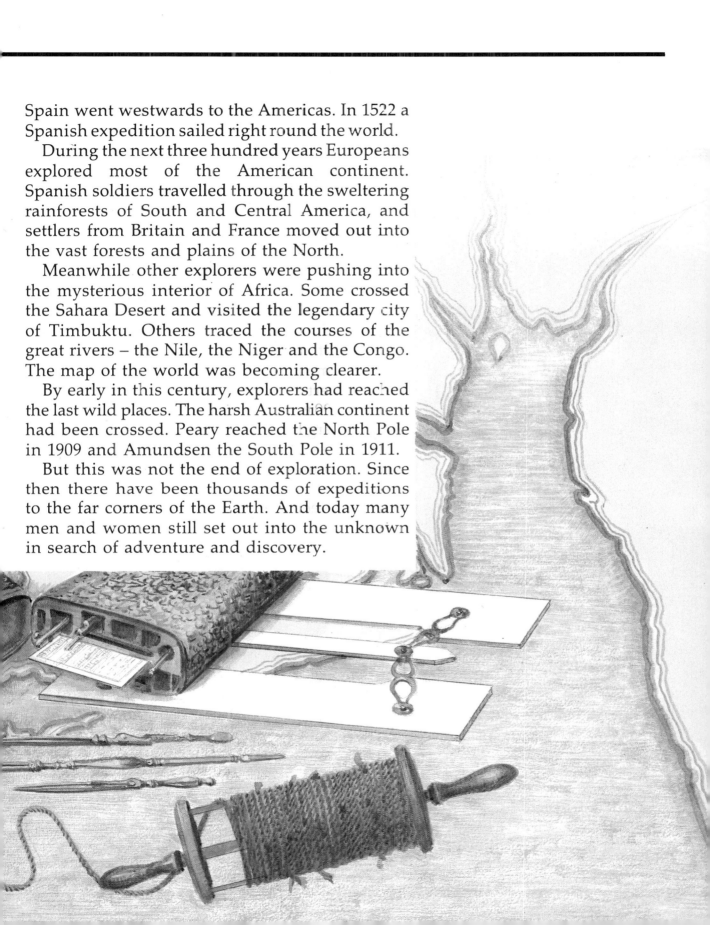

Spain went westwards to the Americas. In 1522 a Spanish expedition sailed right round the world.

During the next three hundred years Europeans explored most of the American continent. Spanish soldiers travelled through the sweltering rainforests of South and Central America, and settlers from Britain and France moved out into the vast forests and plains of the North.

Meanwhile other explorers were pushing into the mysterious interior of Africa. Some crossed the Sahara Desert and visited the legendary city of Timbuktu. Others traced the courses of the great rivers – the Nile, the Niger and the Congo. The map of the world was becoming clearer.

By early in this century, explorers had reached the last wild places. The harsh Australian continent had been crossed. Peary reached the North Pole in 1909 and Amundsen the South Pole in 1911.

But this was not the end of exploration. Since then there have been thousands of expeditions to the far corners of the Earth. And today many men and women still set out into the unknown in search of adventure and discovery.

1
Marco Polo

Marco Polo's father and uncle were merchants and also adventurers. In search of trade they travelled the huge distance from Venice to China. There they were presented to the mighty emperor, Kubilai Khan. When they came home they had many wonderful tales to tell.

In 1271 the Polo brothers set out for China once again, taking young Marco with them. The journey was long and dangerous. They overcame illness, fought with bandits, struggled over the high mountains of Asia, and finally crossed the arid wastes of the Gobi Desert. At last they reached the great empire of China.

Kubilai Khan, the ruler of China, soon saw that the young Venetian was clever and hard-working. Marco learned four local languages and Kubilai sent him all over China to report on how the people lived.

Marco Polo saw many marvels on his travels. The Chinese had invented printing. They could tell the time by water clocks and make fireworks with gunpowder. They had also built a Grand Canal, and a Great Wall, more than 2,400 km long.

After seventeen years in China the adventurers were allowed to return home. The journey back was just as difficult as the journey out, but in 1295 the three ragged travellers arrived in Venice. Hidden in their clothes were diamonds, rubies and other precious stones. They were now very rich indeed.

But Marco Polo's adventures did not end there. A year later he was taken prisoner in a war between Venice and Genoa. Whilst in prison he wrote an account of all he had seen in China. This he called the *Description of the World*. It soon became one of the most famous books in Europe. And years later, as he lay dying in Venice, he said, 'I have not told half of what I saw.'

Above *The Polo family leaving Venice on their expedition to China in 1271.*

1254	born in Venice, Italy
1271	sets out for China with his father and uncle
1275	arrives in Peking
1277	Kubilai Khan appoints him commissioner
1292	leaves China
1296	is taken prisoner by the Genoese and writes an account of his journeys
1298	writes his *Description of the World*
1324	dies at home in Venice

Left *Marco Polo and his father and uncle are presented to Kubilai Khan.*

2
Ibn Battuta

Ibn Battuta did not intend to become a traveller. Born into a rich family in Tangier, he trained to be a judge. But like all Muslims he was determined to make a pilgrimage to the city of Mecca, birthplace of the Prophet Muhammed. He set out in 1325 overland across Egypt and the Red Sea.

Immediately he was gripped by the thrill of travelling. He decided to spend as much time as possible in exploring the known world. First of all he made two rules for himself. The first was to visit only those lands which followed the Islamic religion. The second, more bold, was 'never to travel any road a second time.'

He began by studying the lands of the Middle East. He sailed down the Red Sea and travelled by camel caravan to Mecca. He crossed the huge Arabian Desert and travelled on through what is now Iraq and Iran. In 1330 he set off again, down

1304 born in Tangier, Morocco
1325 makes first journey to Mecca
1330 explores the coast of East Africa
1332 sets out for India to visit the Sultan of Delhi
1342 sent as envoy to the Emperor of China
1349 returns home to Morocco
1352 visits the kingdom of Mali in West Africa
c1368 dies at home in Morocco

Right *Ibn Battuta crosses the Sahara Desert to visit the King of Mali, who ruled a great empire in West Africa.*

the Red Sea to Aden and then along the coast of East Africa as far as present-day Tanzania.

Then, in 1332, Ibn Battuta began a much more dangerous journey – to India. There he was welcomed by the Sultan of Delhi, and given the post of judge. He stayed in India for eight years. At last, perhaps glad to be on the move again, he joined an expedition going to China. Somehow he survived through wars, shipwrecks and rebellions, until at last he returned home to Tangier in 1349.

Ibn Battuta had one last adventure. In 1352 he went south, crossed the Sahara Desert and visited the great African kingdom of Mali. He got back to Morocco in the summer of 1354. His travels were over at last. He had covered more than 120,000 km, visited all the Muslim lands and met sixty different rulers.

An illustration from an ancient Persian manuscript showing Arab travellers about to set off on a journey by camel.

3
Christopher Columbus

Christopher Columbus is the best-known of all explorers. But his early career as a sailor ended in disaster. He was shipwrecked! Luckily, he was able to grab a floating oar and safely reached the shore.

He landed in Portugal, far from his home town of Genoa. Helped by the friendly Portuguese, he made his way to Lisbon. Columbus liked Portugal. He married a local girl and studied to be a sailing captain.

At that time the Portuguese were the most adventurous seafarers in the world. Their ships were exploring the West Coast of Africa and returning with many treasures. In 1488 a ship rounded the southernmost tip of Africa. Now the way lay open to the Indian Ocean, and the riches of the Spice Islands (known as the Indies).

But Columbus had other ideas. Instead of sailing eastwards to the Spice Islands, why not sail westwards across the Atlantic Ocean? It had never

Below *Columbus and his men were the first Europeans to visit the islands of the Caribbean.*

been done before and no one knew what was on the other side. Columbus was certain that it would be a short-cut to the Indies. Unlike many people he was sure that the Earth was round.

The Portuguese king scorned his idea. So Columbus went to Spain, where he raised money for his expedition. He set sail from Spain in 1492 with three small ships – the *Nina*, the *Pinta* and the *Santa Maria*. The little fleet crossed the unknown ocean in two months and landed in what we now call the Bahamas, in the Caribbean.

Of course these were not the Spice Islands. But Columbus had proved that the Atlantic could be crossed. In three more voyages he opened up more of the vast continent of America that lay between Europe and Asia, although he always believed these lands were part of Asia.

Because of his belief in a route across the Atlantic to the Indies, Columbus opened the way to the New World. But he received little thanks for his deeds and died in poverty in Vallodolid in Spain.

Columbus presents an account of his great voyage to the King and Queen of Spain.

c1451	born in Genoa, Italy
c1466	becomes a sailor on a cargo vessel
1476	shipwrecked off the coast of Portugal
1492	sets sail across the Atlantic and lands in the Bahamas
1493	second voyage: lands at Dominica, Jamaica and Haiti
1498	third voyage: discovers the mouth of the Orinoco River in South America
1502	final voyage: sails down coast of Central America
1506	dies, poor and neglected, in Spain

4
Ferdinand Magellan

At the age of twelve, Ferdinand Magellan was sent to the Royal Court in Lisbon. Here the talk was all about exploration. Portuguese sailors had sailed around Africa and across the Indian Ocean. They had returned laden with valuable silks and spices. Meanwhile, Columbus had sailed across the Atlantic in a Spanish ship.

Magellan was thrilled by these stories. He joined the Portuguese navy and served in the Indian Ocean and the Far East. But in 1513 he was unjustly accused of treachery and fell into disgrace. There was now no chance of his being given command of a Portuguese ship. Like Columbus before him, Magellan fled to Spain.

He had a bold plan to put before King Charles of Spain. He would sail westwards to the Spice Islands, a route no one had yet found. But how

Right *During Magellan's epic voyage one of his ships was lost in a storm and another turned and fled back to Spain.*

would he get past America? This was simple. He had heard that there was a narrow channel far to the south which would give him passage into the unknown Pacific Ocean.

And that is what he found. He set sail with five ships and 227 men in 1519. After a mutiny and a shipwreck, three of the ships made their way through the channel, now known as the Magellan Straits. Then came the terrible crossing of the vast Pacific. The food and water ran out and nineteen men died. At last they sighted land. Magellan's great plan had worked.

But his triumph was short-lived. After exploring the Marianas and Philippine Islands, he was killed in a battle with the natives. His crew sailed off, leaving behind two of the ships. In the end only one ship and eighteen men got all the way home to Spain. They were the first people to sail right round the world.

Although Magellan was killed before the end of the voyage, his ship the Victoria *returned to Spain with eighteen men. She was the first ship to sail right round the world.*

5
Henry Hudson

By 1600 ships could sail eastwards round Africa to the Far East. Or they could go south through the Magellan Straits into the Pacific. But there was still one route to the East which remained a mystery – the northern route around Asia.

The Muscovy Company of London wanted to find this route. So in 1607 they gave Henry Hudson a ship and told him to search for it. Hudson was then over forty years old and a skilled navigator. He sailed northwards until he reached the Arctic pack ice, then turned eastwards past the island of Svalbard. Soon after, he was blocked by more ice and returned home.

Next year Hudson tried again. This time he got a little further east and crossed the Barents Sea. But once again the pack ice blocked his way. In 1609 he made his third attempt to find the Northeast Passage, in a ship given him by the Dutch East India Company. Storms and ice forced him back yet again.

c1565 born in England
1607 first voyage to find Northeast Passage: blocked by ice
1608 second voyage: again blocked by ice
1609 abandons third attempt and sails to find a Northwest Passage
1610 second attempt at Northwest Passage: finds Hudson Bay
1611 mutineers set Hudson and others adrift: all probably die
1631 ruins of a shelter found in Hudson Bay, possibly Hudson's

Right *The starving crew mutinied during the long winter and set Hudson and eight others adrift in an open boat to die in the freezing Arctic seas.*

However, Hudson did not return straight home. He had heard stories about another way to the East. This lay, not to the North of Asia, but to the North of America. Hudson crossed the Atlantic to America. Here, he found a wide channel. He hoped that this would be the Northwest Passage, but it did not lead to the Pacific. It was a river, still known today as the Hudson River.

Hudson set out on his fourth expedition in 1610. He again headed for the North West. After sailing north of Newfoundland, he found another wide channel. This led to a huge bay, now called Hudson Bay. The expedition was forced to spend the winter in this icy region of northern Canada. The crew mutinied and set Hudson, his young son and seven crew members adrift in an open boat. None were ever seen again.

In 1631 another explorer found the ruins of a shelter on the shore of Hudson Bay. It may have been built by Hudson and his men. He had never discovered the Northwest Passage, which was not found for another 300 years.

Hudson comforts his young son during their last hours.

6
Francisco de Orellana

The Spaniards began their conquest of South America in the early sixteenth century. They came in their great ships in search of treasures – gold, jewels and spices. The native South Americans were no match for Spanish guns and swords. But the wild jungles and mountains were not so easily conquered.

Among these Spaniards was Francisco de Orellana. He was an officer in the army led by Francisco Pizarro. They landed in Peru and in 1535 Pizarro founded the city of Lima. Three years later, he appointed Orellana to be the governor of Guayaquil (now in Ecuador).

Having found all the treasure near the coast, Pizarro sent an expedition inland to find more, and he appointed Orellana second-in-command. The expedition travelled over the high Andes Mountains and down into the rainforest on the other side, where the rain fell solidly for six

c1490 born in Trujillo, Spain
1535 lands in Peru with Pizarro's invading army
1538 made governor of Guayaquil, Ecuador
1541 joins expedition to explore the interior of Ecuador: sets off down the Amazon with 50 soldiers
1542 reaches the mouth of the Amazon and returns to Spain
1546 second expedition to the Amazon: drowned in a shipwreck

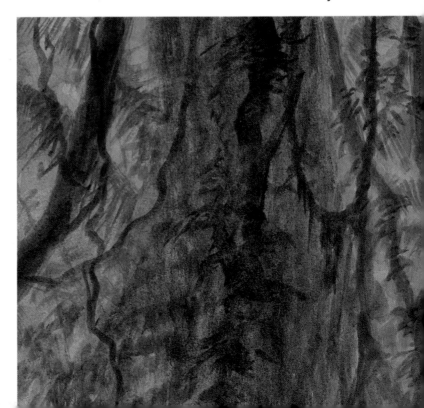

16

weeks. They had to hack their way through the jungle, but they found no treasure.

At last they reached the Napo River. Now the men had to build a ship. Somehow, using timber from the forests, nails from horseshoes and rags from their own clothes, they built one. Orellana and fifty of the men were sent downriver to see what lay ahead. They found a much greater river – the Amazon.

Having reached the Amazon, Orellana decided to carry on down the river and try to reach the Atlantic Ocean. The home-made boat drifted with the current and the crew were attacked by local Indians, who fired poisoned arrows at them from the river banks. Seventeen months later they reached the vast mouth of the Amazon.

Orellana returned to Spain in triumph. In 1546 the King of Spain sent him back to explore the Amazon further. But his luck had run out. On the return journey Orellana's ship was wrecked and he was drowned.

Above *An old engraving of the mighty River Amazon.*

Below *Orellana and his men had to hack their way through the dense rainforest to reach the river.*

7
Vitus Bering

Vitus Bering was born in Denmark. He joined the Russian navy as a young man and became a hard-working seaman, but was no bold adventurer. So he must have been surprised when he was chosen for a special mission in 1725.

Peter the Great, Tsar of Russia, wanted to know more about the far eastern coastline of his giant kingdom. This bleak and icy region, swept by gales and freezing fog, had never been explored. Nor was it known whether Asia and America were joined together.

Bering's task was daunting. He left St Petersburg in 1725. The party had to cross the vast expanses of Russia and Siberia, dragging with them most of the equipment needed for their trip. Then they had to fell trees to build a ship.

At last, in 1728, Bering and his crew set sail up the north-east coast. Cautiously they made their way through the narrow gap between America

Below *Bering's starving men defend themselves against Arctic foxes.*

and Asia, now known as the Bering Strait. Then, fearful of being trapped in the ice, they turned back. At last Bering reached St Petersburg, but the Tsar was still not satisfied. Why, he asked, had Bering not reached America?

So in 1733 Bering began a new expedition. This time it took eight years for the equipment to be transported and for boats to be built. In 1741 the two ships headed eastwards but soon lost each other in the fog, and Bering carried on alone. A month later he and his crew landed on the coast of Alaska. Their job was completed, and now they could go home.

But soon half the crew fell ill. Then the ship was wrecked on an island. Many of the men were dying of disease and hunger, and they were frequently attacked by Arctic foxes. Bering, now an elderly man, died that December. Only a handful of survivors returned to Russia. The voyage had succeeded in its aim, but at a terrible cost in human life.

A dead whale provided a welcome source of meat for the members of Bering's expedition.

1681 born in Denmark
1703 joins the Russian navy
1725 commissioned to explore the seas off north-east Asia
1728 navigates the Bering Strait between Asia and America
1733 beginning of second expedition to survey Asian and American coasts
1741 sets sail in June, after eight years of preparation: August lands on Bering Island: dies there in December

8
James Cook

Young James Cook was good with figures, so his father sent him to learn shopkeeping. But his first love was the sea and at the age of eighteen he became an apprentice seaman. He worked on ships carrying coal across the North Sea, and in 1755 he joined the Royal Navy.

In the Navy Cook quickly worked his way up through the ranks. He proved himself a fine leader and a brilliant navigator. By 1768 he had been given the command of HMS *Endeavour* and sent on a secret mission. He was to search the Pacific Ocean for a huge unknown continent called Terra Australis.

Nobody had explored the whole Pacific Ocean before. This vast area covered nearly a third of the Earth's surface. Some people believed that it contained the mysterious Terra Australis.

Cook landed first on Tahiti, where the inhabitants gave him and his crew a joyful greeting.

1728 born in Marton, Yorkshire, England
1746 becomes an apprentice seaman on a cargo ship
1755 enlists in the Royal Navy
1768 given command of expedition to Tahiti
1769 lands in New Zealand and Australia
1772 second expedition: crosses the Antarctic Circle
1776 third expedition: attempts to find North-west Passage
1779 killed in a fight in Hawaii

Then the *Endeavour* sailed on southwards. Cook found no Terra Australis. Instead he reached New Zealand, which he claimed as a British possession. Then he went on to Australia and took possession of that too. In spite of these two important actions, his voyage was seen as a failure when he returned home in 1771.

Nevertheless, he was soon appointed to lead another expedition. The bold aim of this was to sail right round the South Pole. In this way the Terra Australis (if it did exist) could not be missed. Cook encountered ice and storms but no new continent. On this voyage he became the first person to sail round the world from west to east.

Cook's last expedition, in 1776, took him in search of a Northwest Passage joining the Pacific with the Atlantic. Like many sailors before him, he was blocked by the pack ice. On his way back, he stopped for repairs in the Hawaiian Islands. Here his great career came to a tragic end when he was killed in a fight with the islanders.

A contemporary painting depicting Captain Cook's tragic death at the hands of the Hawaiians.

Below *Cook and his men were greeted joyfully when they first arrived in the South Seas. Later, the joy was to turn to anger.*

9
Alexander von Humboldt

Alexander von Humboldt became fascinated by science early in life. His first interest was botany, and he collected all the species of flowers near his home. Later, he studied rocks, the stars and even foreign languages. All this was a preparation for his main ambition – to become an explorer.

At the age of thirty, Humboldt sailed on an expedition to Central and South America. Being a wealthy young man he could pay for the trip himself. He took one companion with him, a French scientist named Aimé Bonpland. Before them lay a huge continent, most of which had never been explored.

The two men landed on the coast of what is now Venezuela. Early in 1800 they set out to cross the dusty plains inland. Here they came across many strange and then unknown creatures, such as the electric eel. Humboldt and Bonpland caught some of these, though they received nasty shocks in the process.

Below *Humboldt and Bonpland saw many animals unknown to Europeans, including alligators, monkeys and snakes, on their journey down the Orinoco River.*

Now they plunged into the sweltering rainforest. Their food supply was eaten by insects and their clothes rotted in the damp. But the pair managed to survive on river water and wild beans. They travelled by canoe along the Orinoco River, where they saw alligators, turtles, monkeys and a giant anaconda. Then they returned to the coast.

In 1802 Humboldt and Bonpland began their second great journey of exploration. They climbed up into the Andes Mountains and examined the many volcanoes in the range. The highest of these was Chimborazo. Humboldt decided to climb it – without ropes, oxygen or any other special equipment. Although he did not quite reach the summit he got higher than anyone before him.

After returning home, Humboldt began the huge task of writing about everything he had seen. His expeditions provided a great deal of information about the geography and wildlife of South America.

The party rests beside the Orinoco River and Humboldt studies some of the local plants.

1769	born in Berlin, Germany
1799	sails on expedition to Central and South America
1800	crosses the plains of Venezuela and explores the Orinoco River
1802	explores the Andes and climbs near summit of Mount Chimborazo
1804	returns to Europe and settles in Paris
1827	runs out of money and returns to live in Berlin
1829	journeys to visit the mines of Russia and Siberia
1859	dies at home in Berlin

10
Meriwether Lewis and William Clark

Meriwether Lewis and William Clark were both born in Virginia in the USA. They were frontiersmen, skilled at hunting and living in the wild. They had met while in the army, fighting against hostile American Indians.

Lewis went on to become private secretary to President Jefferson. The President's dream was to find an overland route across the American continent to the Pacific Ocean. At that time very few white men had explored the western part of North America. Jefferson wanted to send American settlers to the West to farm these rich and unknown lands. In 1801 he chose Lewis to lead an expedition to the West.

Lewis appointed Clark as his second-in-command. After long preparations, the party of thirty soldiers and hunters set out from St Louis in 1804. They travelled up the Missouri River in flat-bottomed boats. On the way, Lewis made a treaty

Below *The expedition use their dugout canoes to navigate the wild and narrow waters of the Columbia River.*

with the Sioux Indians, and smoked a peace-pipe with them.

Soon the river grew narrower, and the travellers built dugout canoes to carry them. The party had two new members – a Canadian guide and his wife, who was a Shoshoni Indian. By 1805 they had reached the Great Falls of Missouri. The next barrier was the great range of the Rocky Mountains. Fortunately the Shoshoni guide had been born in this region. She knew the paths, and was able to buy horses from a local tribe of Indians. Once over the Rockies, the party took canoes down the wild waters of the Columbia River. At last, in November, they saw the Pacific Ocean before them.

Lewis and Clark's great expedition had been a complete success. They had travelled over vast tracts of unexplored land. Lewis was later made Governor of Louisiana, but was tragically killed in 1809. Clark became Superintendent of Indian Affairs and helped to keep peace between Indians and white settlers until his death in 1838.

Lewis and Clark reach the Great Falls of Missouri.

1770	William Clark born in Caroline, Virginia, USA
1774	Meriwether Lewis born in Charlottesville, Virginia, USA
1801	Lewis appointed by President Jefferson to lead expedition to the West
1804	the party sets off up the River Missouri from St Louis
1805	they cross the Rocky Mountains and reach the Pacific Ocean
1806	returns to St Louis
1809	Lewis killed in Nashville, Tennessee
1838	Clark dies in St Louis, Missouri

11
Burke and Wills

In 1860 Australia was still largely unexplored by its white settlers. None of them had managed to cross the huge continent from South to North, though many had tried. So the government of Victoria organized their own expedition. It was to be well stocked with food and the best equipment. The travellers were to ride on camels, well suited to desert journeys.

But the organizers made a grave error in choosing Robert O'Hara Burke to lead the party. He had only lived in Australia for seven years. He knew little about the harsh country to the north and nothing about exploration. His second-in-command was William Wills, who was equally unsuited for the job.

The fifteen members of the expedition were cheered out of Melbourne in August 1860. From the start, Burke showed himself to be a bad leader. He quarrelled with the other members, eight of whom left the party. New men had to be recruited from local farms.

1820 Robert O'Hara Burke born in County Galway, Ireland
1833 William John Wills born
1853 Burke emigrates to Australia and becomes a policeman
1860 expedition leaves Melbourne to attempt the crossing of the Australian continent
1861 February: Burke and Wills reach the north coast
April 21st: they return to Cooper's Creek
June: both die of starvation
September: last survivor, King, found by a rescue party

Burke now decided to leave most of the expedition members behind, and continue with only four. They reached Cooper Creek, the half-way point, in October. One of them, Brahe, was left here with most of the stores. The rest struggled across deserts and swamplands until at last they reached the north coast in February 1861.

Now came the terrible return journey. They had little food left and were forced to kill some of the camels for fresh meat. In April, starving and ill, they staggered into the camp at Cooper's Creek. But Brahe was not there. He had given them up for lost and set off southwards to join the rest of the party.

Burke, Wills and King (the only other survivor) carried on without food and water. By the end of June, Burke and Wills had both died. King was rescued and looked after by local Aborigines, and in September a search party from Victoria found him, still alive. The expedition had achieved its aim – but at a terrible cost.

Above *Nearing the end of their ordeal, Burke, Wills and King struggle on without food or water.*

Below *Only one man, John King, survived the terrible return journey back from the north of the continent.*

12

Samuel and Florence Baker

Sam and Florence Baker first met in Hungary in 1859. Sam was then thirty-eight years old. He loved adventure and had already roamed the world. Florence was a beautiful seventeen-year-old who had been captured by Turkish invaders and was about to be sold as a slave.

When Sam saw her in the slave market he was filled with pity. He immediately bought her out of slavery and the pair set out on a life of adventure together. Their first expedition took them to Egypt. They travelled down the River Nile to meet John Hanning Speke, who was searching for the source of that great river.

Speke told them that he had found a river flowing out of a huge lake in the south (Lake Victoria). He had followed the river northwards, and had proved that it was the Nile. The river's source had been found, and an ancient mystery had been

solved. But there was another puzzle. Did the Nile flow into another lake after Lake Victoria?

The Bakers decided to search for this new lake. During the gruelling journey they both suffered from malaria and Florence collapsed with sunstroke. At last, in 1864 they saw the lake glittering before them. Sam named it Lake Albert, after Queen Victoria's husband. On the return journey they suffered from disease and hunger and had to cope with angry crocodiles.

Sam and Florence made one more trip to Africa. In 1869 Sam was sent to annex the Nile Basin area of behalf of the Egyptian government. The aim of this expedition was to stop the slave trade and bring peace to the region. Backed by his small band of riflemen, he established a stronghold and defeated a local chieftain.

The Bakers returned to England in 1873 and lived peacefully in Devon until Sam died at the age of seventy-two. Florence died twenty-three years later.

Above *Samuel and Florence travel by camel across the Egyptian desert.*

Below *The Bakers' expedition is lashed by torrential rain on Lake Albert.*

13
Henry Morton Stanley

Henry Morton Stanley was born John Rowlands, in Wales. He never knew his father and was abandoned by his mother when he was six years old. He was brought up in a workhouse and later became a wanderer. In 1859 he made his way to America, where he had the good fortune to meet and be adopted by a rich merchant, Henry Stanley, whose name he soon assumed.

After many adventures, Stanley became a journalist. One day in 1869 his employer gave him a simple order: 'Find Livingstone!' David Livingstone was the most famous explorer of his day. He had been missing in Africa for nearly five years. Stanley set out to find him.

He left Zanzibar in 1871 with a huge amount of supplies, carried by over 200 porters. They made their way through swamps and scrubland to the village of Ujiji. There Stanley saw a frail, white-haired man. Walking up to him, he said:

1841	born John Rowlands in North Wales
1859	goes to New Orleans, where he is adopted by Henry Stanley
1871	sent to Africa to find David Livingstone
1873	explores Lake Tanganyika
1875	second expedition to Africa: sails round Lake Victoria
1876	follows the River Congo over 2,400 km to the sea
1886	final expedition to Africa to rescue Emin Pasha
1904	dies at home in Surrey, England

Right *At Ujiji Stanley nurses David Livingstone through a bout of fever.*

'Doctor Livingstone, I presume?' The two explorers grew to be fond of one another and together they explored Lake Tanganyika. Then they parted and Stanley returned home, while Livingstone, now re-provisioned, remained.

On his second expedition to Africa in 1875, Stanley was determined to solve the mystery of the source of the Nile. He took a boat which was assembled on Lake Victoria, and he sailed right round the Lake. He found one outlet, which Speke had discovered eleven years earlier.

Now began an even more dangerous part of the trip. Stanley and his companions set off to follow the River Congo to the sea. They were attacked by local people and their boats were battered by rocks in the river. But in the end they reached the sea, after a 2,400 km journey.

In 1886 Stanley went to Africa for the last time, on a rescue mission. The mission was a failure but Stanley returned a hero and settled down to quiet retirement in England.

The historic meeting of Stanley and Livingstone at Ujiji in 1871.

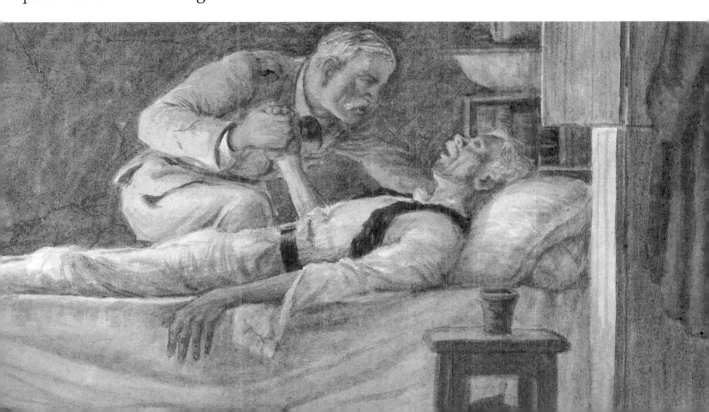

14
Paul Du Chaillu

Paul Du Chaillu was an explorer famed for his zoological findings which included describing an animal new to Europeans – the gorilla. As a boy growing up on the east coast of Africa, he must have heard stories of the many strange creatures to be found inland. After attending school in Paris, he returned to Africa. He became a trader, carrying goods to West Africa. There he heard reports of a huge hairy animal, said to be half-man, half-beast.

Du Chaillu went to live in America and became a writer. But he could not forget those wonderful tales. In 1855 he set out for Gabon in Africa, determined to find – and if possible, to catch – a gorilla. Nobody else in Europe or America believed that such an animal existed.

Du Chaillu made his way into the dense rainforests of Gabon. Later, he wrote an account of this dangerous journey, in which he described

c1836 born on the island of Reunion, east of Madagascar
1852 educated in Paris
1854 becomes a US citizen
1855 expedition to Gabon to search for the gorilla
1859 returns to the USA, where his findings are scorned
1864 second expedition to Africa: sends home gorilla skulls
1901 goes to Russia to study the life of the peasants
1903 dies in Russia: his body is shipped back to the USA

Right *Du Chaillu photographs a family of gorillas to prove the fact of their existence.*

his many adventures, and his fears – of cannibal tribesmen, huge snakes, and the ever-present danger of an attack by a gorilla.

At last he caught sight of the legendary beast, which he described as a hairy giant with huge arms and fiercely glaring eyes. He described how, with an unearthly roar it moved towards the party. They raised their guns and shot it, and several other gorillas as well. When Du Chaillu returned to America and Europe he took many gorilla skulls and skins with him.

But many people refused to believe his story. They said his skulls were fakes. So Du Chaillu went back to Gabon to try and catch a gorilla alive. Although he failed to bring back a live one, he took many photographs of the animals. No one now could doubt his word.

Du Chaillu became a successful writer. But he continued to travel and in 1901 he went to Russia to see and write about the conditions of the peasants there. Two years later he died.

These fearsome-looking but gentle animals live today in diminishing numbers in West Central Africa.

15
Mary Kingsley

Few girls have spent a quieter childhood than Mary Kingsley, who passed her time almost entirely in her parents' home in Highgate, London. She never went to school but stayed in the house, looking after her mother. Her father was often away on expeditions abroad. Mary grew up into a shy girl who was not interested in parties or social life. Instead she was fascinated with science and travel in exotic places.

It was not until she was thirty years old that she was free to go abroad herself. In 1892 her parents died. Mary was now an independent woman, able to do what she wanted, and a year later she boarded a boat bound for West Africa. She landed on the coast of what is now Angola, and then followed the course of the River Congo upstream. With a small band of African porters she travelled inland, living on local food such as cassava and plantains.

1862 born in London
1892 death of both her parents
1893 travels to West Africa to explore Angola and parts of the Congo River
1894 returns to England with specimens of beetles and fishes
1895 second voyage to Africa: travels up the Ogooué River
1897 publishes *Travels in West Africa*
1900 dies while nursing sick prisoners of war in South Africa

It was a most unusual way for a single white woman to behave in those days. But Mary loved Africa; its jungles, its scorching plains and its people. When she returned home, she brought with her specimens of beetles and freshwater fish, which she took to the Natural History Museum. England, however, seemed a dull, grey place, and she soon began to plan a new expedition.

In 1895 she was back in West Africa. This time she went to Gabon, where she travelled up the Ogooué River. The people here belonged to the Fang tribe, who were cannibals. Mary was not in the least frightened. She learned to paddle a canoe in the fast-flowing river, and collected many rare fish. The tribespeople were amazed, for she was the first white woman they had ever seen.

After more adventures, Mary returned to England, where her book *Travels in West Africa* became a bestseller. In 1900 she sailed to South Africa to nurse Boer prisoners of war, but sadly, she caught the disease typhus and died.

Above *A mission station on the Ogooué River in Gabon, where Mary travelled on her second expedition.*

Below *Mary Kingsley is welcomed by members of the Fang, a cannibal tribe that lived in West Africa in the 1890s.*

16
Roald Amundsen

The young Roald Amundsen knew exactly what he wanted to be when he grew up: a Polar explorer. As a teenager he trained hard to become an expert skier. Later he joined an expedition to hunt seals in the Arctic. In 1897 he sailed on an expedition to Antarctica.

Six years later Amundsen took charge of an expedition. He sailed to the Arctic pack ice and then travelled by dog sled to the North Magnetic Pole. Returning to his ship, he went on through the Bering Strait and landed in Alaska. Thus he became the first man to navigate the Northwest Passage.

The voyage brought him fame. But it also brought something more important – a lesson in how to survive in ice and snow. Amundsen learned much from the Inuit, and bought from them warm clothes made of seal and reindeer skin. Now he prepared for an attempt to conquer the North Pole itself.

Below *Amundsen used teams of dogs to haul his sledges to the South Pole, unlike members of Scott's expedition, who hauled their own sledges and died in the attempt.*

Amundsen and his party set sail again from Norway in 1910. Most people thought they were going to the Arctic, but Amundsen had changed his mind. The North Pole had already been reached by the Americans Peary and Cook, so he decided to head for the South Pole instead. This meant that he was now taking part in a race, for a British party led by Captain Scott was also on its way to Antarctica.

Next Spring, Amundsen and four men set off on dog-sleds. They reached the Pole in less than two months. The journey back was even quicker, and not a man was lost. By contrast, Scott and his men pulled their own sledges. They ran out of food and all died in the snow.

In 1918 Amundsen returned to the Arctic and sailed through the Northeast Passage along the Siberian coast. In 1926 he flew over the North Pole in an airship. Two years later he set off in an aircraft to look for an Italian pilot lost in the Arctic and was never seen again. He died in the snow and ice where he spent so much of his life

The Norwegian flag is planted firmly at the South Pole. One of Amundsen's team takes measurements.

1872	born in Borge, Norway
1897	joins expedition to Antarctica
1903	begins voyage to sail through Northwest Passage
1910	leaves on expedition for North Pole: goes instead to Antarctica
1911	becomes first man to reach the South Pole
1918	begins voyage to find Northeast Passage
1925	attempts to fly over the North Pole in an airship
1928	disappears over the Arctic Ocean while searching for a missing pilot

17
Ernest Shackleton

As a boy, Ernest Shackleton longed for adventure. He joined the Merchant Navy and for the next ten years sailed all over the world. But, like Roald Amundsen, he longed to visit the icy wastes of the North and South Poles.

Shackleton's first chance came in 1901 when he joined Captain Scott's expedition to Antarctica. (This expedition failed to reach the South Pole.) On the way back to base Shackleton fell ill and was sent home. This shameful experience made him more determined than ever to get to the Pole himself.

In 1907 Shackleton led his own party to the Antarctic. Leaving his ship at Ross Island, he set off with three others towards the Pole. They took no dogs, and had to haul their sledges most of the way. It was exhausting work. Finally, when they were only 156 km from their target, Shackleton decided to turn back. He had gone further south than any other explorer.

Shackleton was disappointed at his second failure. It seemed worse, in 1911, when Amundsen became the first to reach the South Pole. But now Shackleton had a new plan; to travel right across the continent of Antarctica. He set sail in the

1874	born in Kilkea, Ireland
1901	joins Scott's expedition to Antarctica
1907	leaves London on second attempt to reach the South Pole
1909	gets near to Pole but forced to turn back
1914	3rd expedition: an attempt to cross the whole of Antarctica
1915	the ship *Endurance* is crushed in the ice and sinks
1916	after an epic voyage, reaches South Georgia and rescues all his crew
1922	dies of a heart attack on voyage to the Arctic

Right *The* Endurance *is crushed in the ice, leaving Shackleton and his men stranded. They drag their small boats over the ice to the open sea.*

Endurance in 1914 but his ship was caught in the ice. Slowly it was crushed and sank, leaving Shackleton and his men stranded on the pack ice.

There now began an epic sea journey. The men dragged their three small boats to the open sea and made their way to a bare, windswept island. Then Shackleton and five others took the strongest boat and sailed more than 1,100 km to South Georgia, the nearest inhabited island. Crossing mountains and glaciers, he eventually found help. Thanks to his courage, everyone in the party was saved.

Shackleton died when making yet another expedition, this time to the Arctic. He still thought of himself as a failure. He had not reached the South Pole or crossed Antarctica. Yet he is remembered today as one of the greatest of all Polar explorers.

Shackleton (extreme left) and other polar explorers are photographed at a base camp in Antarctica.

18
Sven Hedin

By the age of fifteen, Sven Hedin had decided to become an explorer. He was small and had weak eyesight, but he prepared himself well for his future career. He learned to speak seven languages, studied map-making, and trained his body to withstand the cold by plunging naked into snowdrifts.

In 1894, Hedin journeyed to the borders of the mysterious land of Tibet. After travelling through the high mountains, he set out to cross the Taklamakan Desert. During this terrible journey the party ran out of water and one man died. Hedin and a companion struggled on for three days, through burning heat and sandstorms. They found a riverbed, but it was dried up. Near to death from thirst, Hedin at last saw a pool of water and they were saved.

Hedin was not put off by this near-disaster. Three years later he returned to the Taklamakan Desert and crossed it. This time it was winter and

Below *Water at last! Hedin and his companion finally reach a pool after their terrible crossing of the Taklamakan Desert.*

he travelled by river, but his boat became frozen into the river, so he and his men continued the journey on foot. In the desert they discovered the long-lost city of Lou-lan, half-buried in the sand.

There was another, secret, part to Hedin's plans. He was determined to enter Tibet and reach the city of Lhasa. No outsider had ever been to Lhasa, which was closely guarded by Tibetan soldiers. Hedin crossed the border, disguised as a Tibetan priest. But he was discovered by a patrol and sent back.

Hedin returned to this area in 1906. This time he managed to trick his way across the border. He spent the next two years exploring the mountains and mapping the rivers in this unknown country. His greatest moment came when he reached the source of the great Indus River.

Hedin's journeys brought him fame. In 1926 he was invited to China to make a survey of roads, but this was his last adventure. He returned to Sweden and lived there until his death in 1952, neglected and forgotten.

Lhasa, the capital city of Tibet. Hedin's greatest ambition was to reach this city, which was forbidden to European travellers in the nineteenth century.

1865	born in Stockholm, Sweden
1894	explores borders of Tibet and crosses the Taklamakan Desert
1898	crosses the Taklamakan Desert by boat: discovers lost cities
1901	attempts to reach Lhasa: expelled by Tibetan troops
1906	second expedition to Tibet, mapping rivers and mountains
1907	discovers source of the River Indus
1926	surveying expedition to China
1952	dies in Stockholm, aged 87

19
Freya Stark

Freya Stark became used to travelling from a very early age. While still a baby, her parents carried her in her basket across the Dolomite Mountains in Italy. When she was four she tried to run away to sea with only a penny in her pocket.

When she was thirty-four Freya Stark began to travel alone. She had learned to speak Arabic, and decided to go to the Lebanon, where she would live as simply as possible. She was later thrilled by her first sight of the deserts of Arabia. In 1929 she made a second journey, this time to Baghdad in Iraq. She shocked British residents there by going out into the desert and staying with Bedouin sheikhs. Even worse – she dared to enter the Muslim mosques!

Stark decided to earn her living by writing books about her travels. In 1931 she set out across Persia (now Iran) to Teheran. Her aim was to find the ruined castles of the long-dead sect of

Below *Freya Stark rides ahead of her guide on her expedition to find the castles of the Assassins.*

Assassins. Although she took a guide, she usually rode far ahead of him. She said 'I always travel alone and I am not frightened.'

Her most famous adventure began in 1935, when she sailed to the Yemen. At that time few Europeans had travelled into the interior of the country. Freya Stark was probably the first European woman to do so. She rode on a donkey to the desert valley called Hadramaut (meaning 'Death is Present'). Then she turned southwards through rugged and dangerous country. On the coast she narrowly escaped being shot by Yemeni villagers.

Stark was awarded the Founder's Medal of the Royal Geographical Society for her desert travels. In the 1950s, she made a series of trips to remote parts of Turkey. She went on foot, by car, or on horseback. Although she was alone, she was disappointed by the lack of danger in Turkey. Stark continued to travel until she was well over eighty years old.

The wild and rugged country of Arabia, scene of some of Freya Stark's best-known expeditions.

1893	born 31st January in Paris
1927	travels alone to Lebanon: first experience of the desert
1929	travels to Iraq and Persia (now Iran)
1931	crosses Persia to Teheran, also alone
1935	begins journey across Yemen to Hadramaut and back
1943	awarded medal by the Royal Geographical Society
1952	begins explorations of Western and Southern Turkey
1984	retires to Asolo, Italy

20
Thor Heyerdahl

As a young man Thor Heyerdahl loved wild places. He went on long skiing and walking tours in the Norwegian mountains, and dreamed of living on an island far from civilization.

Heyerdahl's dream came true in 1937 when he went to the remote Pacific island of Fatu Hiva. It seemed a perfect place to live, but the islanders did not welcome him. His food ran out, he fell ill and, after a year, he returned to civilization.

However, while on Fatu Hiva, Heyerdahl had watched the waves that rolled right across the Pacific. Surely, he thought, the waves might carry a boat. This could have been how people had first come to the islands many centuries before. Historians believed the islanders had travelled eastwards from Asia. Heyerdahl wanted to show they could also have come westwards from America.

To prove his theory Heyerdahl built a balsawood raft called *Kon-Tiki*. He set sail from Peru in April 1947. Carried by strong currents and winds, *Kon-Tiki* reached the Marquesas Islands three months later, proving that Peruvian Indians could have settled in Polynesia. Later, in 1957,

his studies of the strange stone statues on Easter Island supported his theories.

In 1969 Heyerdahl began a new voyage. This time his boat, called *Ra*, was built of reeds. He was trying to show that ancient people had sailed across the Atlantic from Europe to America. The first boat broke up in mid-ocean. Heyerdahl tried again in *Ra II* and got safely to the West Indies.

His next adventure ended sadly. He built another reed boat, *Tigris*. He wanted to discover how ancient people had carried cargoes on the high seas. *Tigris* sailed successfully through the Red Sea and the Indian Ocean. But Heyerdahl was angered by what he saw – polluted seas and civil wars. In protest against the bloodshed, he and his crew set fire to *Tigris*.

Heyerdahl's raft Kon-Tiki *is driven across the Pacific Ocean by the winds and tides.*

Glossary

Aborigines The native inhabitants of Australia.

Anaconda A very large snake.

Annex To take possession of land or claim ownership of it.

Assassins Members of a secret sect of Muslim fanatics in Persia in the 11th century, who were sent to murder christians.

Balsa Wood Timber from the balsa tree, which is very light in weight.

Cassava A plant with a large starchy root which is eaten as a vegetable.

Dog sled A sledge which is hauled by a team of dogs over ice and snow.

Dugout canoe A boat made from a hollowed-out log.

Inuit A North American people living traditionally in Arctic regions.

Malaria A disease causing fever and sweating, which is transmitted by the bite of a mosquito.

New World The continent of America. The 'Old World' was Europe.

Northeast Passage The sea route between the Atlantic and Pacific Oceans along the northern coasts of Europe and Asia.

Northwest Passage The sea passage from the Atlantic to the Pacific Oceans along the northern coast of Canada.

Pack ice Masses of lumps of ice floating close together in the sea. Pack ice is found in the Arctic and Antarctic Circles. In winter the water around pack ice freezes over.

Plantain A tropical fruit similar to a banana.

Polynesia Groups of islands in the Southern Pacific which include Tonga, Samoa, Easter Island, the Society, Marquesas, Hawaiian and Cook Islands.

Spice Islands A group of islands in the Western Pacific, famous for growing cloves, nutmeg and other spices. Now known as the Moluccas.

Terra Australis A legendary great southern continent which was once believed to exist. Although Australia took its name from this, it turned out not to be Terra Australis.

Tsar The name for the old rulers of Russia.

Water Clock A device for measuring time, powered by running water.

Workhouse Formerly a building where the poor were fed and housed in return for work.

Further reading

Captain Cook by Alan Blackwood (Wayland, 1986)

Columbus and the Age of Exploration by Stewart Ross (Wayland, 1985)

The Discoverers by Daniel J. Boorstin (Dent, 1984)

Explorers by Neil Grant (Hamlyn, 1980)

Explorers on the Nile by Andrew Langley (Wayland, 1983)

The First Men Round the World by Andrew Langley (Wayland, 1983)

Lost Paradise: The Exploration of the Pacific by Ian Cameron (Century, 1987)

Ferdinand Magellan by Alan Blackwood (Wayland, 1985)

Marco Polo: The Travels translated by R.E. Latham (Penguin, 1985)

Scott and Amundsen by Roland Huntford (Hodder and Stoughton, 1980)

Spotlight on the Age of Exploration and Discovery by Leonard W. Cowie (Wayland, 1986)

World Atlas of Exploration by Eric Newby (Mitchell Beazley, 1976)

Index

Picture acknowledgements

Bruce Coleman 33, 41; Mary Evans 7, 15, 17, 19, 21, 23, 25, 27, 31, 35, 37; Mansell Collection 9; Topham Picture Library 39; Wayland Picture Library 11, 13, 29, 43.